Frank P. Angelucci, resides in South Philadelphia, where he has written songs, poetry, and short stories, since his early teens.

POETRY COLLECTION

BY

FRANK P. ANGELUCCI

Austin Macauley Publishers™
LONDON • CAMBRIDGE • NEW YORK • SHARJAH

Ordering Information
Quantity sales: Special discounts are available on quantity purchases by corporations, associations, and others. For details, contact the publisher at the address below.

Publisher's Cataloging-in-Publication data
Angelucci, Frank P.
Poetry Collection

ISBN 9798889105756 (Paperback)
ISBN 9798889105763 (Hardback)
ISBN 9798889105770 (ePub e-book)

Library of Congress Control Number: 2023918108

www.austinmacauley.com/us

First Published 2024
Austin Macauley Publishers LLC
40 Wall Street, 33rd Floor, Suite 3302
New York, NY 10005
USA

mail-usa@austinmacauley.com
+1 (646) 5125767

This book is dedicated to my late wife, Barbara; to my son Frank Jr. and his wife Valarie; and to the love of my life, Peggy.

We Shall See

At the rate that things are going right now
I wonder what to expect
The world is on a crazy course
Making our nerves a wreck

Democracy is being threatened
Politicians just don't care
And elections are in question
People are running scared

Prejudice and sexual preference
Are being purposely ignored
Ignorance and violence
Are growing more and more

Even with all these problems
There is still the hope
That change will come and put us
In an optimistic scope.

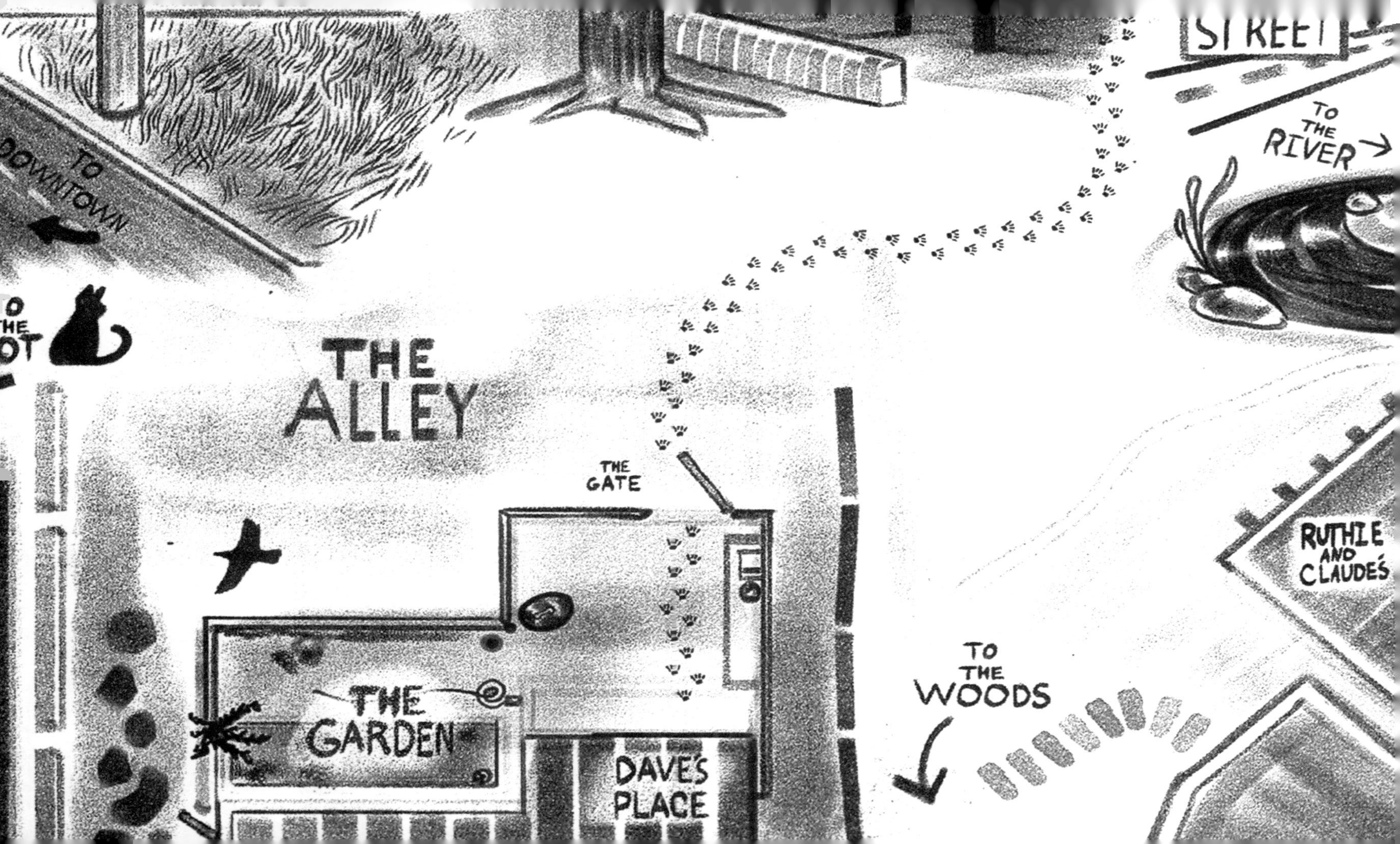
STREET
TO THE RIVER
TO DOWNTOWN
TO THE LOT
THE ALLEY
THE GATE
RUTHIE AND CLAUDE'S
TO THE WOODS
THE GARDEN
DAVE'S PLACE

Dreams

When we close our eyes at night
And we've fallen fast asleep
Our subconscious starts its journey
Into a land so deep

Sometimes our journey is pleasant
Other times, it can be cruel
We have no control over it
Like a tradesman without his tools

They say dreams have a meaning
Just how I do not know
Some people have their theories
And think that it is so

So close your eyes and dream on
May everything be good
Some dreams tend to come true
I hope for you they could.

Time

The past, present and future
Are all factors of time
There isn't a thing that we do
That time does not define

Our time is very precious
We only get one turn
It pays to use it wisely
And live and love and learn

As the years come and go
Swiftly passing by
Get your share of laughter
For sometimes we have to cry

Time is the one thing we have
That we cannot hold it still
So answer opportunity when it knocks
If you don't, another person will.

Much Too Many Commercials

As I sit there with remote in hand
My TV is at my command
Sitting on my recliner chair
Trying to hide my despair

All I see is people telling me
What to eat and where to be
Commercials are coming at a pace
Throwing their products in my face

Trying to watch a movie or show
On regular TV is not a go
Every few minutes they come along
Making my resentment strong

One day I really like to see
When TV is commercial-free
I'm sorry but now I have to run
My favorite show has just begun.

The Old Clock on the Wall

I could remember when I was a child
Looking up at the clock
Watching the big and little hands
And hearing the tick and tock

I used to like when the second hand
Made its trip around the face
I never thought the time would come
When it would lose its place

Today the time is shown to us
In a different sort of way
The numbers now are digital
In all forms of display

Yes, the old clock on the wall
Is soon to be obsolete
And the numbers that I remember
Will never again compete.

Remembering Long Ago

Everyone knows those precious times
That were filled with laughter and glee
And all of the people who made it so
Like friends and family

We all have laughed and we all have cried
Sharing the good times and the bad
But I choose to remember the good times
And all of the fun we had

We've made mistakes along the line
And had our moment of doubt
But we always had people come along
And lovingly help us out

I'm grateful for all the people
Who were there to see me through
And I never will forget them
As I live my whole life through.

Who's to Say?

There are many things that we have to learn
From the second we are born
Beginning with the fundamental things
That we need to keep us going

But as we grow, we begin to doubt
And life's questions fill our minds
And we depend on so-called leaders
For the answers we must find

But who are these so-called leaders
Who claim to know the truth?
Or is it just their opinion
That they think is absolute

Who's to say what's good for us?
And what is truly real
The only thing that I could see
Is to go by how we feel.

Could It Be True?

From when we were children and we were told
Things that were taken as truths
As we grew to adulthood and realized
That they were only stories from youth

Our parents and teachers filled our heads
With so-called historic facts
And we were expected to accept it all
Without any answering back

I guess they did it out of duty
To put us on the right road
But they never thought that one day
Truth would unburden the load

From the Earth's creation to Santa Clause
And all the other telltales
That we carried around for many years
Have come to the end of the trail.

Fact or Fiction

When we think that we have a problem
We must find if that is so
Should we treat it as a problem
Or should we simply let it go?

How do we know if a problem exists?
How could we tell if it's true?
There's a way to know if one exists
And I have that answer for you

Just analyze the situation
And view it front and back
And ask, is the present situation
Fiction or a well-known fact?

Our thoughts could be very deceiving
They could form a solid conviction
But we could combat that deception
By deeming it fact or fiction.

But What About You?

So you say that my behavior
Isn't quite up to par
You think I will be better
Being where you are

You simply can't imagine
How I go about my day
Doing all the wrong things
That's totally not your way

But I wonder what would happen
If you came face-to-face
With the fact that you're not perfect
And you too have falling grace

When you criticize others
Wishing they would change
Take a good look at yourself
What would you rearrange?

Why Do We Get Old?

This question has been raised
Many times before
The answer isn't simple
For it varies more and more

We get old because we fail
To stay in touch with youth
We can't adjust to the change
That life deems as the truth

Laughter and love have become
A thing that only once was
The topic of conversation is
Sickness and what it does

We get old because we think it so
Because age has made it clear
Instead of enjoying the time we have
We wait for death to appear.

If Only There Was Love

As I look around me, I see the faces of
Uncertainty and woe
All that they seem to dwell on
Is misery pain and sorrow

They constantly talk of the past
Those precious good old days
Very rarely do they smile
When thinking of present day

Instead of positive thinking
Their heads are full with doubt
They rarely welcome happiness
Wandering aimlessly about

I say welcome sunshine
And smell the lovely flowers
Enjoy God's precious blessings
Until our final hour.

Pray

When someone we love is visibly ill
And anxiety takes over our life
What else could we do but give our all
To ease the stressful strife

When all of our efforts seem in vain
As the problems quickly mount
Just try to put them in the hands
Of the only one who counts

The one who eases our aching hearts
The one who takes all of our pain
And shows us the way to a blissful solution
And makes life seem carefree again

Yes, The Lord is our refuge and our friend
All we have to do is pray
He will do whatever it takes
To bring us a better way.

What the Mind Allows

It's amazing, all the things we hear
In the silence of the night
And all of the things that appear
That are really not in sight

The wandering mind could sometimes be
An enjoyable happy ride
But the wandering mind could also be
A place for pain to abide

Anxieties and fearful thoughts
Will live inside our heads
When we allow worry to win
We create the things we dread

It's up to us; we have the choice
Do we want to be happy or sad?
It all rest in our inner thoughts
Life could be good or bad.

Mrs. Orland/Mrs. Cowan

You've tried to help me
Yes, you did
But I was just
A selfish kid

You gave me a chance
To change my scene
But my mind was
Always in a dream

My thanks to you
My lady bosses
Who unfortunately had to
Take your losses

I guess you will never
Ever really know
How I appreciate
You trying so.

The Bully

You wake up in the morning
With dread inside your heart
Wishing that the day would end
Even before it starts

Going to school is such a chore
As anticipation takes its toll
The bully's going to be there
Taunting and harassing your soul

You pray that he's not in today
In fact you wish him dead
All the punching, ridicule and hurt
Are fresh in your aching head

But your hopes are shattered quickly
For you see him as he stands
Smiling as he greets you
Making his demands

Yes, it's just another day
Of misery and pain
Looking for ways to avoid it
But here it goes again.

Innocent Lies

We've all one time or another let our
imagination run
We've made things happen that were never done
We've told a story that was partially true
But left some things out and made up
something new

Our ego sometimes makes us tell what we
like to see
Although untrue it sounds so good, it just has
to be
When we hear someone else's story and wish it
happened to us
We will steal the glory and savor all the fuss

Often we are insecure and think that our life
is no where
We must somehow find a way to cover
up our despair
So what we do is exaggerate or alternate the facts
And hope that no one will ever find the truth that
we held back

So when we find ourselves telling those captivating
innocent lies
Just bear in mind that sometimes the truth will
eventually start to rise
When telling someone something that we want
them to know
Think a minute and ask yourself: Would you believe
it's so?

A Child's Memoir

You've helped me go through a time
That was so hard for me to bear
You probably didn't even know
All you had to do was be there

You had no idea how I felt
Or how I dreamed of you at night
You probably would have laughed out loud
If you saw me hug my pillow tight

It's been many years but I still regret
Not ever revealing my heart to you
But I was just a very young boy
Who didn't know what to do

I want to thank you very much
For you just being who you were
I don't know if I could have made it through
Those two years you made a blur.

Being in Love

No words that I could say
Could express what I feel inside
When you look at me that way
My heart takes off on a joyful ride

When you smile, fairytales come true
And life is so worth living
All the sweet emotions that I feel
Makes me grateful for the love you're giving

I'm never sad when you're around
You make me feel so good
Your very name's a beautiful sound
You make all things seem as they should

You, my love with your many charms
And your lovely way of showing me
When you're holding me in your arms
How wonderful love could be!

It's That Kind of Day

The morning sun shining through
The fluffy white clouds
The sound of children in the yard
Playing and laughing out loud

The birds are singing pretty songs
The trees are full and tall
Flowers are blooming everywhere
OUR LORD is giving His all

People are smiling and saying hello
As they come walking by
Mother Nature's magical show
Is pleasant to the eye

Lovers are walking hand in hand
Happy in every way
Filled with peace and security
Yes. It's that kind of day.

Questions

What made you become so mean?
And hurt us like you did
Why did you opt to be so cruel
Especially when you were our kid

What did we do to make you turn
So destructive and full of hate?
Why did your family suddenly become
Your victim of such an ill fate?

What made your heart become so cold
And abandon all those who cared?
You purposely ruined your parents' life
And caused so much despair

After many years and so much pain
Forgiveness has shown us how
To put behind those very sad days
And to concentrate on now.

That Precious Moment

It happened in a wonderful place
One you will always remember
It happened on a beautiful day
Sometime in September

The sun was shining bright above
And the birds sang lovely songs
As you kissed beneath the shady tree
True love came along

You never thought it could happen
That love could take your heart
But as you stared into those eyes
You knew you must never part

As you hear the music play
Even though no music is there
You hold your lover in your arms
And whisper that you care.

To Be That Man

Over the years, I've had the vision
Of what I wanted to be
A teacher or writer or poet
Perhaps I could be all three

But so far it hasn't materialized
At least not this minute
But I will give it all I have
To assure that I get in it

Someday I will reach my goal
And realize my dream
It's going to take some time I know
And a lot of work it seems

When I get to my point of success
And I'm doing what I should
My happiness will surely shine
And all things will be good.

Yes, We Need the Bad Things Too

If things always went our way
And we never had a care
If everything was always good
How would we compare

If tears never filled our eyes
And our hearts had never ached
We would never know the joy
That only love could make

If rain and snow never fell
And clouds were always nil
How would we appreciate
The absence of winter's chill?

Always remember in times of woe
That comes our whole life through
Take a little time to think
We need the bad times too.

She

She didn't know who was following her
As she walked the deserted street
She didn't know the tragic fate
She was about to meet

She never saw the devious grin
Plastered on his face
She never heard the footsteps
Keeping with her pace

She never turned to look behind
Her focus was straight ahead
She was thinking of her warm abode
And getting into bed

She never knew what hit her
As she went tumbling down
She never felt the pains of rape
As she lay dead on the ground

She never saw her loved one's tears
At the funeral on that dismal day
She never knew that murdering scum
Was never made to pay.

That Bloody Trail

The night is quiet; it's after ten
The rain has stopped; it's clear again
Father and daughter are walking to the car
He starts the ignition but doesn't go far

All of a sudden comes that awful sound
Of many bullets being sprayed around
After they stop, the father lay dead
With two of the bullets lodged in his head

The daughter cries out holding her chest
With blood running down her fingers and breast
The ambulance comes like many times before
Making this killing number 154

The daughter survives but in her mind
The nightmare lingers for a long, long time
The shooters are caught and thrown in jail
As the saga continues down that bloody trail.

25

The End

When a loved one is sick or in pain
We get a feeling that can't be explained
There's that inadequate feeling that we find
When the solution is far from our mind

The look in her eyes pleading to you
Desperately wanting relief to come through
All you could do is suppress the tears
As you remember all those wonderful years

You watch as she looks so helpless and sad
The doctor's prognosis is nothing but bad
Your hope seems to be growing thin
But your faith is making you strong within

Suddenly she looks peaceful and content
She looks at you; her love is sent
With a smile on her face, she looks away
And she closes her eyes and closed they'll stay.

Why Not for Me?

They say that freedom of speech is for all
A right for which we fought for
We've earned the right to say what we think
Whether we are rich or poor

I really don't think that applies today
At least not as far I could see
If I should say what I really feel
The censors will jump all over me

Why not be honest and admit the truth
That freedom of speech is rapidly fading
And is limited to a chosen few
Without regret for degrading

Facing the truth could be very difficult
Sometime contradicting what we were taught
But the consequences are much too great
And cannot be sold or bought.

We've Had Our Turn

I watch the children outside my door
Playing without a care
At first I envy their worry-free time
And then I realize that I was there

We all have our time of childhood bliss
When all the decisions are made for us
We all have our time of protective love
And everyone for us makes a delightful fuss

But then comes the day that we must face
When life makes its demands known
And we are the one whom it's demanding from
And our strength and courage must be shown

So when we watch children at play
Just remember as we yearn
For those glorious and carefree days
We too have had our turn.

No More

You see the rage in his bloodshot eyes
As he violently slams the door
You try to run but he swings his fists
And knocks you to the floor
As you cower in a corner
The blood running down your face
He's calling you degrading names
As your heart continues to race
Suddenly you find yourself
Climbing to your feet
You stand and look him in the eye
And you dare him to repeat
He takes another swing at you
But what he doesn't see
Is the knife you have in your hand
That ends his wife-beating spree.

www.ingramcontent.com/pod-product-compliance
Lightning Source LLC
Chambersburg PA
CBHW040113150726
48005CB00013B/1689